How to Avoid the Pitfalls and Hype of Social Media and Online Marketing!

While Increasing Your Revenue Almost Instantly...

I0469137

The Guide to YOUR Profit Revolution!

Discover Forgotten Marketing Tactics Your Competitors are Completely Oblivious to and Avoid "Following the Crowd" by Smartly Using Proven, Measurable, and Almost Instantly Profitable Strategies...

by RANDY GAPPEN

DEDICATION

This book is dedicated to Larry and Joan Kreisberg who, without their love, support, and in-your-face reality checks, I wouldn't be the man I am today... and without which, I seriously doubt I would have had the courage to start a project like this nor the tenacity to finish it.

I also dedicate this book to all of my former students in my economics and American government classes who helped me grow in more ways as a person than they'll ever know. You proved the teacher-student relationship is unbalanced... for I, as your teacher, learned far more about myself and developed so much more as a person from you, compared to any lesson or instruction you received from me. You know who are, Thank You

Lastly, and most importantly my daughter Micaela and my son Lucas who are the light of my life and give me passion, reason, purpose, and the desire to be the best father I can be, which is the most precious gift a man can ask.

CONTENTS

ACKNOWLEDGMENTS

I have been blessed by the wisdom and friendships from the following people who have helped me immeasurably in becoming the man I am today,: Coach Mike Dau of Lake Forest College, Lake Forest Illinois by first planting the marketing–copywriting seed by insisting the most important skill a person can learn is to become an expert at communicating with the written word. Later suggesting I should pursue a career in advertising. Bob Dunn, my guidance counselor senior year at South Plantation High School, Plantation, FL who revealed after being interviewed many times for the school newspaper, my writing was the first to time someone conveyed what actually felt in an article.

Prof. Bill Moskoff, Lake Forest College, Lake Forest, Illinois for being the first person in my life to acknowledge, support, and "go to bat" for my ideas and decisions. Art Lieblich, haberdasher "extraordinaire," who taught me the value and importance dressing like a professional, looking good, and appreciating nice, well made "classic style" clothing. Fayne Johnson who gave me my first shot at teaching English to adults who had no inkling of how to speak English.

Real Estate investing "Guru" Ron Legrand whose courses I devoured, seminars I attended, only to discover I hated real estate investing but through Ron I learned about direct response marketing and more importantly, discovered Dan Kennedy.
I am eternally grateful for discovering Dan Kennedy, whose marketing and copywriting expertise has changed my perception of myself, my business, how I see money and view wealth, and even my spiritual development.

Former E-Diets CEO and founder, and co-inventor of the supermarket scanner, Dave Humble, who welcomed me into his home, opened my eyes by obliterating the "greedy rich" stereotype portrayed by the mainstream media and simply confided in me his passionate and fascinating entrepreneurial stories and the lessons he learned from them. We both agreed that sometimes venture capitalists take a good business and run it mercilessly into the ground.

Craig Cadwalader, who shared with me his fears and concerns after the 2008 market crash over the future of not just his business, but the business climate in general. His honesty, compassion and humaneness further helped in deconstructing my misconceptions of the wealthy and financially successful. A fellow dedicated reader, he made some wonderful recommendations as well.

And lastly Andrew Cass and Mande White of South Florida Renegade Marketers, my mastermind group, who have influenced me more in just 5 months, than they'll ever know... and our relationship is just beginning – you two look, marrrvelous, simply marrrvelous.

1 YOUR MARKETING: WHY IT'S BROKEN AND HOW TO FIX IT

"I am NOT a thought leader... in fact, I'm not sure what a thought leader is."

Randy Gappen

Howdy, I'm glad you're here. I'm glad because you're open enough to look at something most people would rather delegate to someone else: their marketing.

The thought of it stirs fear and loathing in the hearts of most businesses and business people, yet it is *the* most important function of any business. No marketing, no clients. It's that simple. But just because you do market doesn't mean its paying for itself and generating any return on investment. Have you ever thought of your marketing as an investment. Yes? No? Maybe? Have you ever considered your marketing and sales process to be a valuable asset that generates healthy returns for your business, year in and year out? Does it bring in enough new business? Reactivate lost accounts? Maintain contact with current clients?

And now your *supposed* to blog, create "killer" content (for free) on your social media sites in the hopes that some influencer somewhere in cyberspace will... well, will "like" what they see and then tell their friends how great you are. This new age of marketing logic is devoid of one key thing - anybody buying or trying to sell anything.

Which is why I wrote this book. Most (by most I mean at least 92%) of the marketing put out by big firms, web consultants, and yes even techies in the form of SEO consultants, is completely useless. It's created and designed to display the ad agency's, creative, artistic, and writing skills and talents, not make your business money.

Several years ago, I read where the ad industries most prestigious award, the Caple's Award, in honor of the late, legendary ad man, John Caples, who himself was a tremendously capable salesman with the printed word, eliminated the requirement an ad had to achieve any sales at all to be eligible as a finalist... it just had to be clever, funny, and creative. Not sell anything! So why are marketing firms and ad agencies in the business of promoting clients' products in the first place? Good question and... I don't know.

It's no different than the Super Bowl ads everyone gets so worked up over with anticipation at the end of each January. They're creative, some make you laugh, some you might even be lucky to remember months later. But they all fail in one significant area; they don't sell anything. Sure, one year a kid sucked himself through his straw into the bottle of Pepsi he was drinking.... it was new, creative technology, people thought it was "cool" but were you compelled to buy Pepsi after seeing that ad? This year was no exception except it seemed fewer ads were funny and creative and technical animation (the fish swimming and singing around a new premium style of Beck's Beer) were the order of the day. No selling, just visual stimulation and the self indulgence of advertising agencies illustrating both their creative abilities and their woefully pathetic inability to engage someone to buy something.

Is Your Business Guilty of Blindly Following "Accepted" Truths About Marketing?

The other day I was at the gas station filling up and talking on my cell phone. The woman who was parked on the other side of me was walking up to her car from paying and she looked at me aghast with fear. She said, "You know it's very dangerous to speak on your cell phone at the gas station. Your phone can emit a spark and cause the entire place to blow up." I looked at her and said "What?" not showing any signs of concern or fear of her comment. She looked at me indignantly and hurriedly got into her car and drove off.

I never heard that one before, so onto google I went and low and behold, that particular urban legend was born about a year and a half ago and disproved about as quickly as it circulated around the web. This woman apparently didn't get the memo.

Unfortunately, most business, like the woman I rand into at the gas station, hang on to ideas and beliefs about their marketing and advertising as if they're reliable, solid, widely accepted truths just like cell phones causing gas stations to go up in flames. They simply haven't gotten the memo about what works and what doesn't in marketing their business, product, or service. What I'll reveal to you is what really works in marketing that gets staggering results which drive enormous profits.   To some it sounds "too good to be true" and "get rich quick".   My hope is to show you why it's neither one of those things but actually based on sound principles, most writers, advertisers, and online consultants aren't even aware of.   In fact, in our 15 minutes of fame culture today, and all the hype we're exposed to that quickly flames out, the principle I'll disclose turned 100 years old in 2012.   They continue to work, quietly yet spectacularly for those who are "in the know" and aren't afraid to put them to use.

But first, you'll learn "the way things are done around here" because "that's the way everyone's always done it" of what I refer to as traditional marketing. Glossy ads, few words or print, cute slogans, or the ad doesn't even remotely relate to the product its trying to sell (or represent).   You'll also learn why most big companies with huge corporate ad budgets would be better off dropping leaflets over cities with pictures of their product on them rather than use the almighty agencies.

So fasten your seat belts and get ready for an insightful and hopefully profitable ride.

How Direct Response Marketing, both Online and Offline, will Bring Astounding Results, You'll wonder *"If I only knew this stuff years ago"*

The cure, as you will soon discover, harkens back to the age when modern America was in its infancy. Created and perfected by a man who died in 1937 his two works, "My Life in Advertising" and "Scientific advertising" both written by Claude Hopkins, are perhaps even more relevant today than they were more than 90 years ago.... Multitudes of non-traditional or direct response marketers over the years have consistently cited "Scientific Advertising" as their "Bible" of effective advertising. Many commit to reading it annually. Claude Hopkins' classic is what successful direct response marketers use as a baseline and it's why they achieve consistently higher and more profitable results, than traditional "Madison Avenue" marketing and both online and social media marketing. You are about to learn why your marketing isn't getting you outstanding results and what you can do about it.

2 MARKETING MYTHS EXPOSED

"It takes a big idea to attract the attention of consumers and get them to buy your product. Unless your advertising contains a big idea, it will pass like a ship in the night. I doubt if more than one campaign in a hundred contains a big idea."

David Ogilvy

Most people in business have no idea how to market or sell. That's all marketing really is... selling. Most people are terrified to sell and unfortunately judge selling as somehow sleazy, dishonest, or "beneath them." There's a huge stigma against selling and the funny thing is it's something all of us do, not necessarily well by the way, each and every day.

In fact selling is not taught in most MBA programs in our nations universities. Most companies still rely on sales and marketing tactics in their sales training programs from 30 or more years ago, where the marketer or sales rep is more of a hunter, a stalker trying to "get the sale." Everybody knows these tired, stale, ploys by now and resents and resists sales and marketing messages that sound "familiar". It's evolved to the point to where it is socially acceptable to be rude to sales and marketers, lie to them, negotiate with them, and even curse at them.

Jim Koch, founder of Boston Brewing Company, which brews its now iconic Samuel Adams lager, recalled the moment he had to go out and promote the first batches of Samuel Adams. He had recently resigned his post at McKinnsey and Company as a consultant, to start a local brewery based on a recipe a distant relative and founder of the country, Sam Adams. He had, up until the first batch of Samuel Adams was available, never sold anything before. He only had to walk around the corner from his office to a local watering hole. He carried a small cooler with several bottles of cold Sam Adams. As he approached the door, he hesitated... feeling queasy, his palms started to sweat, and he walked through the front door. Behind the bar was the bar owner, looking up asked, "can I help you?" "I have some samples I'd like you to try of my beer". His voice quivered nervously. He poured a bottle for the pub owner. He took a sip. "I'll take six cases" he said.

Leaving the bar, orders in hand, Koch recalled feeling, triumphant, elated, light on his toes, on top of the world and most importantly, never felt that kind of fear and elation simultaneously before and such a sense of victorious accomplishment after.

The Ad Man's Prayer

There's a prayer in the ad agency business that my mentor, Dan kennedy refers to often. It goes something like this:

"Dear Lord, Grant me one client today, who owns a pet food processing plant and he is blessed to have a wife who owns a white French Poodle"

Cute, but the underlying point of the "prayer" is that if the wife has a white French Poodle, guess what's going on the label of every bag, can, and box of dog food? Right: the wife's white French Poodle. Won't make a hill of beans one way or the other as far as increasing dog food sales. More importantly it reveals the attitude towards creating something unique that will also sell that is missing in most of today's marketing and advertising

Ad Agencies

The advertising industry is full of smoke and mirrors. Most of what they put out is complete garbage. Creative directors are in charge of a lot of what goes or does not go into an ad. Most creative directors have never even written ad copy before. They believe solely in the visual effects that may attract a buyer but not in the writing which will persuade the buyer to buy. It can be pithy, catchy, cute, trendy, or not make sense at all but the one common element of today's modern advertising is that it **avoids selling your product or service!**

If that's true then how can they get away with it you ask? Because nobody else in the business world knows how to market either. Most people see advertising and marketing as this vodoo-like, hokey-pokey, artsy-fartsy way to attract customers because that's what you're supposed to do and they rely on everybody else's bad examples of marketing to create their own.

Ad agencies, on the other hand, are terrified to track the results of their ad and marketing campaigns because of what those results will reveal: their ads totally bombed and were completely ineffective. Then they'd be exposed and held accountable for their results. Being an ad agency is like being the President of the United States. If the economy goes up, the President get's the credit, but if it falls, the President takes it on the chin. Same for an ad agency. If the client does really well, then its the ad agency's brilliance. If the client does poorly, well unlike the president, the ad agency tries to deflect blame to the economy, the client's customers or some other arbitrary factor; but *they* were not at fault.

This has been going on since television came of age and advertising turned more "visual". This was just a natural evolution but what was lost was the writing to sell. It has slowly evolved into advertainment - hoping someone will remember your product because of how cute, funny, clever or entertaining the commercial or advertisement was.

Hope is not a strategy.

This really is a case of the blind leading the blind and as time marches on, you'll be playing a vicious game of merry go round with agencies as you hire, fire, and re-hire agencies trying to find one, just one, that can deliver half decent results.. But as sales copywriter John Francis Tighe used to say, *"In the land of the blind, the one-eyed man is king"*

Web Page Designers

Web designers are good at one thing: getting your website to at least function. That's it. Now you may say, "hey Randy, take it easy here... what are you writing a hit piece on all of your competitors?"

Let me explain...

Web designers are technically oriented, engineer type, linear thinking people. Now, I'm not judging them, that's just the way they're wired. They truly are techie's with a *slight* creative bent.

Their focus is creating cool, neat, websites loaded with bells and whistles that don't have any ability to attract more clients or sell clients on doing business with you once they get to your site. They're there to show - off the web designers talent and include what *he* thinks is important to attract clients. Now, they can definitely build websites, that function on the web that deliver your company's message to your clients and even set up a web store for you but they can't get you traffic and they can't effectively attract people to your business's site. Here's an example of a proposal from a local Web Design/SEO firm. See if you can make heads or tails of this proposal and ask yourself if you'd feel comfortable signing on the dotted line.

SEO Consultants

SEO or Search Engine Optimization is a hot topic of debate right now because of the 800 lb. gorilla in the room: Google. I'll get to why that's important to the health of your business in a minute. In the meantime, an SEO consultant's job is to make your site easier to find on google by essentially "pleasing" Google.

How?

By building your sites online presence in a way that Google approves. This is called organic growth. It simply means to Google that your site has developed naturally by having back-links to legitimate blogs or websites that relate to your business or industry. It also means you have content on your site that helps solve current problems for potential clients without expecting anything in return.

Sounds o.k.... right? I mean, what could be wrong with that?

Nothing is necessarily wrong with it, you just have to realize what's behind organic SEO building to decide if your company should invest resources in mastering it. Not only that, done correctly and ethically, it should take about a year to achieve consistent page 1 ranking. A lot of factors contribute to achieve this and is really a book by itself. The resources section at the end of this book will give you the information you need to get started on the right path or to test your current efforts and tweak any weaknesses you might discover.

But... and this is a BIG but, anything you do on Google, is *dependent* on Google. And Google has a way of frustrating advertisers and marketers who rely solely on them to spread their company's message.

Google uses a complicated algorithm designed to foil spammers and black hat SEO writers (people who can get you on page one of Google by building fake traffic and links to your site.)

Google updates its algorithm sometimes twice a year, so nobody can "crack the code" and decipher the algorithm and figure out how to gain page 1 rankings instantly. What this means to you is that one day you could have a top ten ranking on page one of Google one day, and immediately following an update, your website is nowhere to be found. Google has a lot at stake here. They defend their turf from spammers and "junk" because users don't want to be bothered with

See, what a lot of people don't realize about Google or Facebook is you don't own anything that you post on either site. Your content is, well... their content in a sense. So the question you got to ask yourself and business partners is how much of your marketing do you want to expose to a media that can shut itself down randomly, anytime it wishes, without any regard to how much money you lose because your clients can no longer find your site.

For online marketers this is a very vulnerable position to be in, as recently documented in July when Google released their updated algorithm, Gorilla, sent many online business owners scrambling to locate their sites and frantically regain first page listings. Going from thousands of dollars in sales a day to ZERO at the flick of a switch is not a position I would envy to be in.

Why Direct Response is THE Answer

Soon (like next chapter soon) your going to learn why most marketing fails miserably and what you need to start becoming aware of so you can stop blowing wads of your or your company's cash on the latest provoking online trend hawked by some social media "thought leader."

You're also going be to exposed to the *forgotten tactics* of smart, client oriented, and profitable marketing. They're called forgotten tactics because, well.... they have been forgotten by most Madison Avenue agencies for close to 50 years and never even made into university B - school marketing curriculums... so this is great stuff. Thanks to Claude Hopkins's astute observations and tenacious efforts during the late 19th and early 20th centuries, you are fortunate enough to now be exposed to the extreme profit making principles of direct response marketing.

Direct response means exactly that: the person you are trying to sell your product to, has to respond in some way to your marketing showing their interest or essentially raising their hand saying "I'm interested." As you will see, this is a sane approach to acquiring more of your best type of clients rather than trying to be all things to all people.

3 THE **BIG** REASON

"Enough about me, how great do you think I am?"
Hollywood actor's joke

All About You and NOT your client

One of the chief reasons your marketing fails is you focus entirely on you... and not your client or prospect. It's not your fault; you're only doing what you see everyone else doing. Don't worry they haven't got clue what to do either.

Put yourself in your client's shoes. Do you really care how long some establishment's been in business? Or that they're on Facebook, twitter, and Pinterest now? Or you're family owned, employee owned, have your own fleet of service vehicles and have been awarded the best place to work, have the best customer service, and Vice President Joe Biden made two campaign stops during the last campaign?

I think you get the idea. No wonder customers aren't loyal - nobody is speaking to them in words *they want* to hear - nobody's speaking *their* language.

Stop and think about it for a minute... who are your favorite people, merchants, customers, companies, etc. to do business with? I'm willing to bet dollars to donuts that they're the people who pay the most attention to *your* needs.... they're the one's who earn your business. What can you do to correct this huge faux-pas nearly 98% of all businesses make?

You can start by asking yourself these 3 questions:

•   Who is your ideal client?

•   What keeps your ideal client awake at night?

•   Why should your ideal client choose to business with you over all other available alternatives to you?

Just who is your ideal client anyway? Do you know? You're in good company because most people have no idea. Its usually more like anyone that has a pulse that needs what we sell. Not a good answer by the way.

How do you find out? Simple... and it will probably take less than an hour. The ol' Pareto Principle in action. I know you've heard of this principle, and maybe you never really thought it would apply to your situation.

Well it does. And in a dramatic way. Look at your revenue generated last year. Look closely. What you'll find may startle you... in a good way. 80% of your previous years revenue was generated by 20% of your clients.

How's that for basic math?

So that means you can afford to fire the 80% of your clients who only divvy up 20% of your business. Before you start breaking into a cold sweat about firing clients who've been "loyal" for years, keep this point in mind. If they're so loyal to you and your business why then are they only giving you token business and giving somebody else 80% of their business they should be giving you. Have they *earned* the right to be your client? Do you really want to be the one who your clients view as the company of last resort?

In one of my previous lives, I was a financial advisor with one of the major firms in the industry. My mentor, Tim, who helped train me was a former large accounts rep for FedEx. He said saying no to clients and refusing to be 2nd fiddle not only earned him respect... it was company policy.

Thing is, the shipping business, like many businesses, is commoditized to a certain extent. Clients who shipped a lot and could shave off a couple of pennies here and there could potentially see huge savings by the end of the year. So a competitor of FedEx's simply played low ball and clients would switch to the competitor and use FedEx when they were in a jam.

When Tim noticed a major accounts volume drop, he'd pay a visit to the CEO to see what was going on. The CEO was usually blunt and said in order to save costs, we've decided to use your competitor and his company would just use you "in case of emergency." Tim didn't have a problem returning the serve in a match of hardball. He'd simply say, "O.K.... I'm pulling the account and you can no longer do business with us until you return to your previous volume."

He recalled to me how CEO's would always scream angrily "You can't pull the account, because I'm the CEO!!" He would calmly reply with his stock answer , "I just did!"

It would only take a matter of weeks before the competitor screwed up enough times to make it inconvenient and costly. The disgruntled CEO invariably would call Tim sheepishly (and eating crow) asking to have their accounts reinstated.

If FedEx can do it, why can't you? Taking away your business or service from a client eliminates being taken for granted.

Do you remember the scene in the movie Twilight Zone, where Dan Ackroyd said, "Do you wanna see something really scary?" In your case it will be doing something scary - try calling those 80% clients and honestly ask them why they don't more business with you. Do you really want to know?

Or just you could just fire them just as easily because you, your staff, your operation is wasting time, energy, and money serving clients who don't pay or in other words if you broke down your ROI per client, you could very well be losing money on the time and energy spent servicing these accounts.

It's your money... you decide who you would rather deal with.

Now, in the interest of disclosure, I have to admit, in my early years in sales, I was just as guilty as anybody pleasing every customer no matter who, large or small -

all customers were created equal in my eyes (and they're always right). Boy was *I* ever wrong.

I sold dental supplies in the late 80's and early 90's. I developed some large, multi-partner accounts who would appreciate my service when I went out of my way for them and rewarded me with the bulk of their business.

I had some others who, weren't as loyal, but I would still go out of my way for them in "hope" (there's that word again) they would do business with me.

One dentist, Dr. David, loved to look at samples of dental hand piece diamonds. In layman's terms they are the "drill bits" a dentist uses to drill out a cavity, prepare (cut away part of) the tooth so a new crown or bridge or even a veneer can fit on what's left of the original tooth and the patient can comfortably close their mouth when the dentist is done.

Now Dr. David loved to go through the entire diamond wallet, which was nothing more than a small three hole binder with about 20 pages of diamond drill bits front and back.

Painstakingly, he'd carefully analyze all the diamonds in the wallet, even the ones he wasn't interested in. Then he would choose between 6 and 8 diamonds and place his order. This was not your ordinary order, because these diamonds had to be special ordered and they were, as I recall, only $8.95 - $10.95 each. They were the top of the line luxury brand - the best.

I bet you can guess where I'm going with this story. After waiting 2 weeks for the diamonds, and having them in his office for another two weeks, he returned <u>all</u> of the diamonds. It get's better... I *allowed* this to happen three times.

Schmuuuckkk!!!!!   I finally wised up and ultimately, learn my lesson.

You Don't Have a USP, or Worse, You Have No Idea What USP Is

Does your business or company have a USP? Most don't.   Most companies compete with their competitors as "me too" competitors.   No difference in what they offer except price, color... think of big box retailers like department stores, office supply stores, home improvement stores, etc. You get the idea.

A USP is your Unique Selling Proposition, what is unique about your business that would make someone choose to do business with you over someone else. It has to be clearly defined, easily understood, in just one sentence.

For example: "Fresh, hot pizza delivered in 30 minutes or less - guaranteed"

Since the 1980's Domino's Pizza's USP has been ingrained in our minds because we've heard it so often.

How about this one from the late 1800's, "God Created Man, Samuel Colt Made Them Equal" Not as familiar but if you were alive at the time and living on the plains or in the old west, then you'd recognize the USP for Colt Firearms. The equality message here also subtly infers safety and personal protection.

Your USP is also called your elevator speech. When you get on an elevator and somebody asks what you do, you give them your USP in about 16 seconds. Mine is, "I help businesses frustrated with the lack of results from their online marketing by creating hyper effective marketing solutions that are measurable, accountable, and almost immediately profitable - guaranteed."

What does it mean? For one thing, it means that the solutions I'll provide are measurable, my client and I will be able to quickly see if what I recommend is working or not. Next, if it's not working, well then I'm accountable to fix it, and make dog gone sure that it is effectively bringing in money for my client. Almost instantly means you're gonna see results quick.... and I guarantee it.

What does your company offer... what problem does it solve for your clients? It helps if The Big Problem your product or service solves is the same one that keeps your client awake at night. This will take several times, so be patient. In fact, I've rewritten mine several times over a few months just to get it right.

You Don't Have a UVP - This is a New Idea... So you get a pass for not knowing this one.

This relatively new proposition evolved as a result of the 2008 economic meltdown. The effect of an entire generation's pre-retirement savings evaporating over-night, feeling betrayed by the financial services industry because what they hoped to retire on, in as early as three years for some, had turned not to be safely invested at all leaving most reeling at how carelessly and their investments were handled and the vulnerability they were exposed to.

What do the pre-retirement investments of the baby-boom generation have to do with your unique value proposition? A lot because an industry that was trusted with giving financial advice failed to warn clients of the real risks involved with their investments, causing many to not distrust only the financial services industry but just about everyone they do business with - trust is lost today in business and its harder now to gain it that it has been ever before in our time.

That was also when I started my new career as a financial advisor. The market had recently crashed and investors were understandably shell-shocked. Those who were closer to age 65 were nearly inconsolable. Plagued with fear of doing anything and anger at the traditional "buy & hold" advice everybody gives, investors were at least receptive to hearing what I had to say, but cautious about switching firms for fear of "jumping out of the frying pan and into the fire."

But it was more than that.   The investing public was in disbelief at the size of their losses.   Some lost more than half the value of their retirement assets. How do you earn that back if you're 63 and were planning on retiring in two years?   The investing public felt bamboozled by the investment industry and for two years sat on the sidelines leaving their assets sit idle, hoping that they could recoup their losses.

So your Universal Value Proposition is: *what value do you provide to the market that is unique to you and builds upon the trust of your clients or future clients*? Or another way, how do you position yourself as a valuable resource, so you are considered indispensable by your clients and potential clients, bidding the value of your services higher because the value of what you offer will greatly ease whatever pain your clients face. Andrew

Cass, my Business Coach here in South Florida, recommends a checklist to see how unique the value you provide really is. See how many items from Andrew's list you can check off:

Unique Value Proposition

a.) **Who Are You?** A short 2-3 sentence paragraph explaining who you are... more than just your name

b.) **Where Did You Come From?** What is your background story? Why should we trust you?

c.) **How Are You Relevant?** There is no generic audience; how are you relevant to *your* audience. You must create agreement or *"mutual pain"*

d.) **Why Should Prospects and Clients Pay Attention to You?** Status? USP Question? You Need to Make Apples to Oranges Comparisons which is the path least traveled to differentiation.

e.) **How Are You Casted?** What are you known for; Clarity

f.) **What Do You Do?** Your USP and product/ service benefit driven link.

g.) **Why Are You Doing This?** What is your mission or your company's mission; what's the challenge you are up against? What's your quest? People would rather buy your "mission story" than your product.

h.) **What Are Your Values?** What do you stand for? Who do you support? How can you tap these emotions to obligate your clients and prospects?

i.) **How Do You Sharpen Contrast?** How do you show up differently than anybody else?

j.) **Where's the Mystique?** What is your company's "mystery factor"? What do you intentionally hold back from prospects and clients to sustain interest in your company? Again - Think Apple

Those are the questions Andrew uses when deciding how he is going to create a value proposition for a new product or service he is providing for his clients and prospects.

No Systemized Method of Consistently Attracting Clients

I saved the best for last, the biggie, the numero uno of all reasons why most marketing fails. And it's this: **no system in place to consistently attract clients and run your business.** The great fortunes in this country were built by people who leveraged either themselves or their employees to get more efficiency and more production. Ray Croc took the McDonald's Brother's hamburger stand and systemized the burger making process to make more burgers faster and eliminated the thinking that mires down employees and created processes, when followed, produced a consist tasting burger at every location in the country. It's so systematized, teen-age kids can run a franchise blind folded without even having to think about it.

Henry Ford did the same thing. He invented his first car but had no way to mass produce them. He got the idea of his assembly line from the slaughterhouses. Beef is butchered in along a line and the head of beef is transported throughout the slaughterhouse where a different department would butcher a different section of the cow.

Borrowing this idea, Ford was able to produce his Model T, more quickly and efficiently, catapulting output and revolutionizing manufacturing. But he had a lingering problem. How to distribute his efficiently mass produced automobiles to buyers around the United States? His solution was to allow business owners around the country to share in the opportunity of going into business with him by becoming a dealer. Ford correctly reasoned who else to better sell my cars than someone in a town or city people already know and trust. And the automobile dealership model was born.

Let's recap - what we just discussed. The reason most businesses and business owners fail is because they -

1. Focus on their wants and not their clients needs, so their marketing is boring and prospects just skim past it.

2. Have no idea who your ideal customer is, what keeps them awake at night, and why should they choose you over given alternatives.

3. Fail to have a unique selling proposition and a unique value proposition.

Knowing the answers to these three key things will begin to set the foundation elevating your business head and shoulders above your competitors.   But you're not done yet... we're just getting started.

7 Questions Every Business Needs to Have Rock Solid Answers For.

1. What is your Powerful, Attention Getting "Promise Statement" - The "Benefit" your prospect will get by using you

2. What are you doing to build credibility - reasons why they should listen to you.

3. What Problem-Solution are you using to create agreement: mutual pain you both share and you can eliminate for the customer.

4. Are you making Apples - to - Oranges comparison between what you market and your competition? It is the path least traveled to "Differentiation" and "Unique Selling Proposition"   How do you differentiate your services without going toe to toe or head to head with your competition and avoid being chosen by price?

5. Do you use a "yes" close in your presentations? i.e"How do you want to title this account, in your name or in the name of your business?"

6. Prescribe... DON'T sell.   More professional and reassuring to the client and you don't sound like everybody else. Do want to be a hunter or a fisherman? A fisherman is what you want because your "bait" or your marketing attracts ideal   p r o s p e c t s   y o u ' v e identified. Also people resist   sales and marketing that is high-pressure   "salesmanship" or the hunter

mentality. Remember: People love to buy, but hate to be sold.

7. Publish or Perish "The" most important thing you can do to increase your credibility is to publish a book that makes you the *obvious expert*. This will establish you as an expert in your field or business or industry, and price resistance to what you offer will melt away like snow in March.

I should also point out that every marketing message your company puts out, every claim, benefit, or solution has to pass the "so what" test. If, after reading any of your firm's marketing message you say to yourself "so what" then your marketing piece isn't effective. Because if you read "Since 1927 our Acme Wonder Widgets are the greatest thing since sliced bread" and you respond... "yeh, so what" then you have work to do. We'll get to more of how to apply this test later on in the book.

4 ONLINE MARKETING RE-DUX

"We don't know who invented water, but we're pretty sure it wasn't fish"

Marshall McLuhan

Too Many Choices?

If you've ventured into the online arena recently for marketing then you know how overwhelming it can be. Just about everybody is online these days. Whether its a website or CRM software auto generating email sequences to prospects, the web has really changed the way people do business. Probably the best advice I've come across in regards to doing business online comes from Perry Marshall in his book the Ultimate Guide to Facebook Marketing. He says, "If you want to build a real business that makes money, most of the the money you find in social media books demands enormous amounts of manual labor from you at best. And much of that advice is woefully ineffective. If you want to build a real business that makes money, invest $1 in advertising, acquire a customer, and get $2 back." In fact, the big 3 advantages of using social media search, content, and reach, can all be handled through Google Ad Words and a well written web page.

Email - Avoid Being a Spammer

Unfortunately... its too late for that because spamming has altered the way we use and view email. Like an annoying television commercial, email in many instances has become a crutch for some marketers and annoyance to the people they're trying to meet. So is there any way you can effectively use email to reach prospects without your message being diverted into trash or a spam filter? According to Jeff Walker, creator of the Side Ways Sales Letter, the answer is a resounding yes! How? By launching your product or service to a list of only 200 - 300 people. Why? Launching your product or service on email positions you as a market leader or guru. This is ideal for both current clients and new clients.

You basically invite your current clients and/or new prospects to a call and simply ask them what are their top 3 problems they face in the market today relative to what your product or service solves and what could you do to solve their problem. The answers you receive from this call (which you record) create your next product or update an existing one.

According to Jeff, the interaction of an email sequence providing a lot of beneficial and useful content to your prospects and clients is the key way to develop your product for them. Walker also says the email sequence cuts through the "marketing fog" that afflicts all of us. We're just inundated with marketing messages from the time we get up to the time we finish, sending out your new product launch in 6 timely email sequences turns your marketing into an event. Not much unlike Apple when they unveil a new IPhone or IPad or

Microsoft's updated version of windows. You can have the same impact on both existing and new clients as well.

The impact on your clients and prospects occurs because you are focusing on hitting their mental triggers throughout your email campaign or pre-launch. The most powerful triggers are:

a.) Authority

b.) Reciprocity

c.) Community

d.) Anticipation

e.) Conversation

f.) Scarcity

Trust with your clients and especially new prospects is high because you giving actual, usable content they can benefit from. By giving good, valuable content, you build up trust and authority because you don't fear giving away valuable information for free.

"Our website is just not living up to our expectations"

If your website isn't living up to your expectations there's a couple of things you can do to make your site attract more clients. First, what are doing to drive traffic to your site? Is there another online push, like ad words, or an email blast, or a link from your landing page that can drive more traffic to your landing page? See the biggest problem is most websites are written by techies and they don't know how to sell. They're great at making your site look cool (if that's what you want) or put all kinds of graphics and visuals that represent your product on the site, but they don't encourage the visitor to click through for more information.

Next your site *probably* isn't well written as far salesmanship goes. What do I mean?

Most sites today are just electronic versions of a company's business card, catalog, or resemble an old Yellow Pages ad. Really... be honest. Would you stop and read on yours site if it wasn't yours? Does your site make you want to purchase something? Download a free report? Register for a tele-seminar or webinar to see how your company can solve a particular problem for you prospective clients?

Does your site collect all the contact info of a prospective client and not just first name and email address only? If not, why? Your site is a way for your company to build rapport with future and current clients not just for the sale, but for the lifetime of your client relationship.

If you answered no to any of the above questions, you have some thinking to do about your company's site, its purpose, and how are you going to make it attract the clients you want.

This is not a book on site development...but you need to have a strategy to attract prospective buyers to your site. You may need to have (and I recommend that you do) more than one site dedicated to each niche or market you serve. A lot of businesses either don't think about it, are too lazy, or think they are saving money by having a "one size fits all" site. Don't do it. Besides, think back to the last time you were marketed to with marketing that was kind of related to you but not exactly... how did you feel? Compelled to read it or throw it in the garbage can? If I had to guess, you probably trashed it or deleted it with scarcely a second thought. Do you really want to create that deflating effect of marketing that initially piques your prospects interest and only to leave them disappointed before they get to the 2nd paragraph (if you're even that lucky). Lack of impact because your potential clients don't feel your targeting them exclusively is seen as "ho-hum" and boring will not help bring in new business... that is where your money is wasted in your marketing and advertising.

SEO??? Should You or Shouldn't You?

SEO or search engine optimization gets a lot of attention from online marketers who provide SEO services and business that want their websites on the first page of Google. All SEO really is is an attempt by doing certain things with your site, like having links to other sites or key words that match the phrase in your advertising, video links to You Tube - all in an effort to make Google like you.

It's a tall order... getting Google to like you. What most businesses are unaware of is Google uses an algorithm to prevent spammers from figuring out their algorithm, allowing them to spam "at will" and devalue Google. Google is effective only about 30 percent of the time. The biggest disadvantage for companies that rely heavily or solely on Google as I eluded to earlier is how vulnerable you and your site are when Google changes its algorithm, you run the risk of your site being left "high and dry," no longer on the first two pages of a Google search... especially vulnerable to those whose only source of marketing is Google with a high SEO rank.

According to some social media gurus, SEO is the number one reason a B2B company should be using social media; because search engines drive valuable traffic to their websites.

When it comes to SEO, both quality and quantity of links matter. The better links, the better the page ranking. Higher authority links act like jet fuel to amplify the impact to produce more search traffic in less time. According to Stephen Mahaney and Kristi Hagen of Planet Ocean a SEO consulting firm:

"True online success comes from blending the most effective marketing strategies to create that complete online presence to put your business in front of as many people as possible - getting you the most conversions."

Basically, if you have an AdWords system working well and producing clicks, odds are your system will be profitable in organic SEO as well. The biggest and most important thing to remember is that achieving top page rankings from SEO takes a lot of time (up to a year) and requires patience before you see results.

I don't know about you but I've never had any success with making people like me; no matter if it were in business or dating, getting people or Google in this case to "like" your site is setting yourself and your business up for frustration.

Earning Trust

One way I used to try to earn a dentists business was to leave samples of a particular product I was promoting. About this time, the late 80's to early 90's new technological advances in tooth restoration were hitting the market.Now, a dentist could restore a tooth to match the color of the tooth he was restoring - no more ugly, grey fillings. It was a major improvement.

Fresh out of college, I assumed, and the manufacturers endorsed, leaving product samples behind to allow the dentist to "give it a try" before they committed. I was leaving samples all over Palm Beach County, Florida. I thought, "hey, I'm a nice guy. I left them some samples to try. They should like me for doing that and easing their fear of trying a new product for their practice.

Eager to see how many dentists I left samples for actually tried it, I was shocked!!! And disappointed. ZERO dentists had tried my samples. I had the gall to think that over the next two weeks all these busy professionals would be trying my samples and place orders for them once I "followed up" two weeks later. I was stumped, but, I learned my first and perhaps greatest sales and marketing lesson: people do not respect or care about anything, unless they have skin in the game. From then on I stopped leaving samples so when a doctor asked about trying a sample of anything I demonstrated I would smile and say, "No I don't have any samples today Dr. Hinsley, but if your order the into-kit, try it, and are unhappy with it for any reason, I'll refund your money." Sold. It was much easier, much faster, and more profitable. Hope is not a strategy. Google is similar to the dentists I used to call on. They only care about the companies and services that generate revenue for **THEM**.

Sorry, that's reality. The have no interest where your site ranks, but if it seems artificially high, then they'll take an interest to see how it got there, but they won't break a sweat over you loss of web traffic.

5 SOCIAL MEDIA – A GROUND FLOOR OPPORTUNITY WORTH SKIPPING ?

"Whenever you find yourself on the side of the majority, it is time to pause and reflect."

Mark Twain

Where's All the New Business?

Should you be using social media in your business? That depends. Are you local or national, are you a retail business or b2b? Social media does have some limited uses in business but most businesses commit the sin of "me - too-ism" adding links to their social media pages on their home page because everyone else is doing it seems to be the thing to do without taking a serious look at why they're doing and what results are do they want to achieve.

The expectations of social media and what its supposed to do for your business and how you are to achieve results according to the social media gurus is naive. Check out the eager, naive, childlike enthusiasm in the following quotes from Kipp Bodnar and Jeff Cohen's "The B2B Social Media Book"

"A great B2B social media marketer is a brand journalist who cam crunch numbers to maximize results for lead-gen and calls to action."

Integrate social media and traditional marketing

"Social media is a discovery mechanism - discovery is the DNA of social media platforms. It is social media sharing that is so crucial to driving more new online leads for your business."

"To stand out and maximize content discovery on your site you have to: Be remarkable - create content worth remarking about. "The power of social media is that the remarks made about content are now public and shared with others online. Being remarkable drives traffic and leads to your site."

The proof is in the pudding. If the first quote is true, then it seems to be violating the very notion of selling on social media. The second instance sounds like "fluffy thought leader" talk. The besides DNA what I find unnerving is the belief in the continued sharing of free on social media that somehow drives prospect to your site. I was waiting to be empowered and have my voice heard but alas there was only dead air. Lastly, being remarkable in social media seems like a misuse of your company's resources. Their are other, far more important priorities to be remarkable in than social media content. Customer service for instance - do you have systems in place so your employees know how to answer the phone and interact with your clients? How about follow up on leads? Do you have a system in place to "touch" your prospects weekly? All the marketing and advertising in the whether print, digital, or social media isn't worth a hill of beans if your people on the inside can't or won't execute what you want them to do.

Jed Alpert, in his book, The Mobile Marketing Revolution suggests the "shiny effect" of social media has basically allowed people to BS themselves into not focusing on what really matters in marketing - new clients and increased profits - which, he says, is a violation of the Martha Stewart Rule: "Throw your own party don't just cater someone else's"

Alpert goes on to report how the success of Vitamin Water in 2009 caused its site to crash and came back online with their updated site but this time on FaceBook. It crowdsourced development of its new soft drink to its Facebook Fans. They were encouraged to vote on flavors, ingredients, packaging, flavors and naming for the the new drink with the winner receiving a $5000 prize. So far so good, right? But like we've all heard over the years, "but wait, there's more"

Fans were asked to participate in quizzes and games to see which vitamins were needed most. Not only that, fans could submit ideas for packaging and naming the new drink. The winning name was "Connect" and Vitamin Water even celebrated this by putting the Facebook logo on the bottle.

Ecstatic with all of the online participation, the company declared the campaign a success, a winner. Fans increased from 400,000 to 981,000 in just a month and 1.3 million fans by the time of the product launch for the "Connect." Social media pundits crowed at the success of the new product launch and dubbed it a "brilliant success" that "spoke for itself." Really... you don't say. Success at what, exactly?

Social media pundits, bloggers, and "gurus" frequently regurgitate "brilliant successes" of companies promotions that increase Likes and comments from raving fans. So where's the problem? Well, if you base your social campaigns or promote your product and services through social media sites, you'll certainly get attendance but you won't get sales and the data shows that's both hard to convert and contain these non-committal web folks. You'd be better off owning your own marketing efforts and the data those efforts produce.

Did you ever notice that the people want to sell you the idea of "influencers" portray themselves as influencer themselves....coincidence? I think not.

What's happening is some companies feel social media is a replacement for traditional forms of marketing or at the very least, a replacement for the way people connect with each other.

Pfui... social media is just that, a media to be used by a business, if results warrant it. Companies jump onto the social media bandwagon hoping to be heard. As direct marketing mentor and guru Dan Kennedy decries, "Hope is not a strategy". Like any other marketing media, thought has to be given to the outcomes you want, not just to be heard.

Business has become so obsessed with page views, page rank, unique visits, past count, and email forwards, it has lost site of what it's really there for - to make a profit and get a return on investment. Take a look at these statistics from DDB Worldwide and Opinion Research. They found a whopping 84% of a typical brands Facebook fans are existing customers. 3% of a brands Facebook fans are new, have never used the brand, but intend to... while 6% of a brands fans NEVER used the product and don't intend to. Forrester research concludes that: "On average retailers report only a small single-digit amount of sales can be attributed to social media." All the hype around social media, leads people to think its something they need to do.

The big idea to remember here is that social media sites users *belong* to that social media site. Any data regarding sales, which pages were most effective, why, can't learn why people chose a particular page over another belongs to the host site. You might have access to some of the data but your wants are trumped by their needs. The use of things like Twitter and Facebook are overhyped and results or potential achieved from using them too often greatly distorted.

Or as Zappos.com founder, Tony Hsieh said in B.J. Mendelson's book "Social Media is Bullshit" "*I think the term (social media) puts the focus on the method instead of the media intent. Ultimately what really matters is connecting with people and most companies haven't figured out how to do that with the telephone yet.*"

Unless there's something to be gained by using Facebook, you really are wasting your time having a page there at all. If your wondering how you determine if you should invest time and money on Facebook go to this website: www.IsFBforme.com. Perry Marshall, author of the Ultimate Guide to GOOGLE AdWords and the Ultimate Guide to FaceBook Marketing admits Facebook has really one "killer" feature to help define ultra-specific niches marketing to people based on personal tastes they listed on their Facebook profiles. You can custom taylor your ad words campaigns to target say, Grateful Dead fans age 45-57 who are software engineers thinking of starting their own consulting firm. I'll go into more detail a further on in the book.

Focus on your site and AdWords campaigns and offline marketing to generate significant above average returns - stick with what's proven to work. Remember, "Liking" your site doesn't mean the "Likers" have any interest in buying your products or services.

Who Said Social Media is Absolutely Necessary?

Social media allows people who are terrified of selling avoid direct contact with other people, so they can hide behind it as a wall and don't have to entertain the thought of asking someone to buy something, when they rather congratulate themselves for being savvy marketers and referring to themselves as thought leaders.

Probably one of the biggest lures of social media is companies think it will be a quick, cheap, and easy solution to all their marketing problems. Although it seems like a no-brainer to set up a Facebook page and a twitter account, taking both live in just a few minutes... unfortunately, that's the only quick, cheap, and easy part. Don't be fooled by the hype.. there's really nothing that's fast, simple, or cheap about a successful social media strategy.

Increasing influence of the consumer through social media content and the decreasing the role of the marketer and primary advertising message is really nothing more than increasing passivity in sales and marketing results with the customer given less reasons to purchase a particular widget and the stubborn, fearful refusal for organizations to learn direct response marketing.

Social media is an activity based on the notions of influence and participation. So why bother when you can create an AdWords campaign targeted directly to your ideal prospect and not have to hope for influence and participation.

Another myth is one of Network value. How efficiently it supports sharing and collaboration is determined by the way in which members are connected. Yeah... right. Again no real measurable value.

My gut feeling is the social media elite don't really have any real business sense or how to acquire new clients with effective marketing. I often wonder, who makes this stuff up? Check this out from Social Media Marketing by Dave Evans, "Social media plays a significant role in marketing and indeed across your entire organization: The conversations that takes place on the social web determines how easy or difficult - your task in driving conversion will be." What??? It sounds as bad as some B-school professor, wearing a tweed jacket with elbow patches, talking about improving commerce by allowing entry level employees having a greater say in management decision making or the "open door" policy for upper management, got an issue?... drop by my office anytime, my time isn't important. In other words - your guess is good as mine.

Evans continues, "There seems to be an excessive amount of worry on how to deal with a 'determined detractor' who is seen as someone who 'plays' an important role in the evolution of markets but none-the-less will not normally be won over and therefore is generally viewed as a participant with whom you will respectfully agree to disagree to disagree and then otherwise care to not engage." Who cares??? This is what the "Thought Leaders" of social media are concerned about?   Besides, if someone is really that pissed off at your company to spend so much time on the web trying to spread bad intentions, they're either unemployed or perpetually angry at everybody and everything.

It reminds me of the time I heard Dan Kennedy reveal why he doesn't do surveys after seminars and trainings.   What he discovered was the people who responded the harshest, ended up being the same people who purchased his product at the end of his presentation. So he quit handing them out. If you weren't buying after 60 minutes of hearing some of his best stuff, he didn't care.

Corporate Executives for the past 10 years felt ROI is a click-to-purchase action. In social media, that rarely happens... it eventually happens but its not an immediate action based on your media (marketing) efforts. In fact, many in the social media community dismiss ROI altogether preferring for the more nebulous term Return on Influence. It almost sounds new age and metaphysical or "kinder and gentler".   And like advertising, the purpose is just as elusive. Why? Because if you measure "Return on Influence" with actual dollars spent to dollars earned then you'd begin asking yourself what a lot of other execs have already figured out - if social media is an expense that doesn't generate any revenue, why are we investing so much of our resources in something that provides little bang for the buck?

"Essential in developing a robust indication of ROI is tracking the measure over time to gauge the effectiveness of specific marketing activities as they relate to your business formulas. Ultimately, if you sort through the data you have - or could have - you can create a reasonable method of ROI. Create a baseline for your activities and a wide range of marketplace scenarios, and then use this data to separate the various contributions of specific marketplace efforts.

This whole notion that using quantitative metrics are "all the same" or "aren't relevant" to social media or vague generalities like "social networks lend themselves to direct participation" really only serves to keep the obvious from being revealed: **The King Has No Clothes**.

The day these "thought leaders" are found out, they're out of a job or at the very least, they got some 'splain'n to do. Now I am creative, but this stuff I couldn't make up if I tried. The Social Media Elite preach "Social media forces a rethinking of branded content: What does it mean when recipients have a hand in the creative process and when the content itself is reduced to its purely informational state?" I'm not sure if I understand the question. But I think I know who does.

Sir Richard Branson warns of actually listening to customers too much as potentially hazardous to your business. His example is of a company that surveyed its clients about what features and benefits clients would like to see in the next updated version of their product. The clients responded and the company got busily to work creating what it thought was everything their clients wanted in an updated version. Their competitor didn't get the memo and came out with a completely new product that clients had never seen before and it completely changed the way people viewed and used the product. The competitors product flew off the shelves. However, sales were flat for the new release of the updated version and now clients were clamoring to have updates similar to the competitors new technology product.

Branson's point is if you are going to introduce something to your clients they've never seen, then asking them what they want, when what your offering will change the way they think about the status quo is pointless, frustrating, and a costly task.

Social Media Evangelists Scott Stratten and Gary Vaynerchuck even go so far as to tell their audiences to look beyond ROI, arguing that not all value is measurable. Huh? Vaynerchuck even tries to arrogantly deflect the question of ROI by asking "Would you like to know the ROI of your mother?" And Stratten is even more snarky, quipping "Every time I hear 'social media ROI' a unicorn dies."

Even more confusing still, social media pundits and gurus break ROI down into two metrics: Hard dollars which is revenue you can track and Soft Dollars are not trackable or measurable. They are sales based on the "personal touch points" that occur through engagement and interaction. Its as if your FaceBook page is a salesperson, there's no real way to quantify how your FaceBook page connects with users... but we all know its important.

The ROI in hard dollar value is very real and can happen all the time for companies that take the time for to address FaceBook marketing strategically. The ROI in soft dollar value is very real too; however, it is very difficult to quantify. You just have to trust its there working for you behind the scenes.

"But when it comes to marketing measurements of ROI and actions, calls to action aren't as important as influencing actions" How do they know if they can't quantify them? How do you trust they are there "working behind the scenes"

Why Focusing on the Cheapest Marketing is your company's "Kiss of Death"

Social media wonks love leads that come from organic sources because they have a lower cost per lead. In organic channels, big companies own the attention paid channels big companies are renting. Reducing paid media is the fastest way to reduce COCA (cost of client acquisition). Most businesses look at marketing this way... cheapest is best. Here's an idea you probably haven't heard: how about spending more or marketing to attract your best clients and then increase your fees to make up for your increased marketing costs? Scary... sure because few people think that way. More profitable... absolutely. But that kind of thinking goes against the grain of just about everyone in marketing, advertising and sales. Check out this quote from a local web site design/SEO consulting firm:

"PPC (Pay Per Click aka Google AdWords) can be used to start to jumpstart and supplement your traffic when the website is initially launched. We can examine this during the development of the DMS. If you elect to use the PPC during the launch and establishment of your website rankings, we can manage your PPC program and coordinate it with our SEO work. By doing this we leverage both PPC and SEO traffic and we can also develop a transition plan to migrate away from or minimize the dependence on PPC advertising"

Unfortunately, this is how about 99% of businesses, corporations, sole proprietors, ad agencies, seo and web marketers see advertising as an expense to be reduced, almost avoided, if you will, even if marketing campaigns are profitable. Why is it so difficult for people to wrap their heads around the concept as well as the math if you have marketing that is generating revenue, then why not spend even more to generate more revenue and leave your competition in the dust because they're too timid and too cheap to spend money on marketing that works.

Even more befuddling, why businesses and companies would accept marketing solutions the marketing company whether print or digital, is any lack of guaranteeing results or measuring results to see if what's offered is working for the client. Check this example out, again from a local web/seo consultant: *"The results from this project depend on many factors including, the amount of frequency new content is published, blogging and social media activity, and the activity of your competitors such as launching new campaigns or increasing their activity, and your level of SEO investment. Consequently, we **cannot guarantee specific results or ranking positions"***

How comfortable would you feel doing business with this company or any company with as reassuring a position as the one above? 'Nuff said.

Lead generation myths with Social Media

Listed below are the common myths or "mulch" that's being put out by the social media pundits and gurus:

- B2B marketers are closely tuned to the behavior, habits and desires of prospects and customers. I wish that were the case

- B2B companies are trail blazers developing and innovating new and existing ones, hire experts within the industry meaning a boost, in the quest for social media marketing success. Similar to the advice Columbus received before he set sail about the dangers of sailing over the edge of a "flat" earth.

The above Assumes your are great at marketing where you do more with less, generate leads for sales teams, short-staffed soccer moms w/less budget - social media is a "lever" to help reduce cost per lead enabling you to do more with less.

•Social web facilitates relationship building throughout sales and marketing cycle to help improve bad quality - you don't say?

The core to FaceBook marketing comes down to really one question: Do you like me? But people only come to Facebook to interact, connecting to with past friends and new colleagues and becoming visible in your community. So to generate a sale on FaceBook you first need to engage your users, which can be unnerving because ultimately you find the answer to that nagging question, "Do they even care about me enough to talk to me and respond to me."

What some companies are finding having a Facebook page requires a lot of time an effort but no hard and fast results. In fact, Complete Idiot's Guide to FaceBook recommends to get the most amount of fans in the least amount of time, is to use FaceBook ads. And... according to the book Likeable Social Media, the top 10 reasons consumers like Fan pages on Facebook are:

#10 For Education about company topics

#9 To learn more about the company

#8 To get access to exclusive content

#7 Just for fun? (Get a life or at least find a hobby)

#6 For updates on upcoming sales

#5 For updates on future projects

#4 To stay informed about company activities

#3 To get a "freebie" samples, coupons, etc.

#2 To show support for brand to friends

#1 To receive discounts & promos.

At least Likable Social Media is honest when it admits that social media cannot make up for a bad product, company, or organization.... it won't lead to overnight sales success, and it is NOT free. Of all the sources I used to research for this book, Likeable Social Media is the most credible because whether intentionally or unintentionally, the author incorporates direct market concepts in company's websites... which you should be doing too.

For instance, Dave Kerpen, explains "in order to grow on social media and develop a social presence, you have to take the time and energy to attract the 'low hanging' fruit' your current customers and other people who know you, to support you." In other words, you need to develop a good ole fashioned grass roots marketing campaign - online.

Likeable continues to get it right by suggesting how to direct the type of testimonials clients would like from their customers by asking 5 questions ... again another direct response marketing tactic adopted for online use. The questions (authors name) suggests are:

1. What would you like to see more of in the community?

2. Who are you inspired by the most?

3. Where is the most interesting place you've usedv our stuff (great question!)

4. Where did you first use our service? (another great question)

5. Why do you like our page?

Another direct response concept Likeable stresses is not immediately trying to "close" the sale right away but rather build trust first, and over time you'll close more sales. "the more valuable content you can share with your fans and followers, the greater the trust and reputation you'll build with them." You could offer a "free" download of a special report, a teleseminar or a webinar all of which have to provide **real** value before you've asked for a single dime. You're also making it easier to say yes because first your prospects are now comfortable saying yes to your free offers. More importantly, the law of reciprocity is in play because you have "given" them something of value free that has positively impacted their life.

But this doesn't mean you should give away the farm, the store, or your soul for the matter. Groveling for a client is unnecessary and unattractive... and not profitable.

INVASION of *the* "Grouponites"

Remember the sci-fi Movie *"Invasion of the Body Snatchers"*? How the aliens from outer space started duplicating people in a small California town. They looked like the residents of the town down to the very last detail but they lacked human feelings and emotions. And some townspeople caught on and insisted that a spouse or a brother or cousin or whoever was not the same person but someone else? That seems to be what a lot of retailers and businesses using Groupon are beginning to find out: the customers they attract through Groupon and its competitor Living Social, don't have the basic "ideal client" traits that a loyal customer that has been nurtured developed over time has. But feedback that's coming back from businesses that have used those services to acquire new clients isn't encouraging.

Word from the street is that Groupon users have developed a reputation for only taking advantage of the particular deal or discount. They are not interested in becoming long-term clients and they reportedly make their intentions clear to the merchants they redeem their coupons to; rather defiantly and rudely I'm told. Guess what happens as these "one and done" good deal only "Grouponites" descend on the hapless retailer who hasn't experienced the mass fury of a Groupon induced sales surge? Their regular, loyal clients become annoyed, the retailer is overburdened by the temporary spike in business, no hope, lasting value, or relationship building because "Grouponites" are truly a cheap and selfish lot out for only one thing: the absolutely cheapest price possible... while alienating regular customers in the process. It's win-lose.

They are examples of groveling for clients. Sure they're great.... for the customer.   Just because its online doesn't mean an idea is a good business model. Groupon's business model was really DOA, but its taken a little longer for it to go the way of the Do-Do Bird. In fact, they've recently entered the "direct deals" market because they're local deals business has fallen off drastically. Groupon's stock as of this writing has sunk to under $4 a share. Oh well, you know what they say, "live by price, die by price."

Let Your Clients Decide What's on Your Site?

So rather than try to show or force a pre-packaged view of what **you** think your fans should see about your company (on a website nobody will trust anyway) you might want to consider the frightening idea of total surrender of control of your message to what your fans are saying and where they're saying it.

The thinking is you increase your likelihood of that someone sees on your site a testimonial from a friend that has already given their stamp of approval on your

product or service. This makes sense especially if you've read customer recommendations on products before you've clicked purchase online. Amazon comes to mind; reading the reviews for me is social proof the product will do what I want it for - friend recommending it or not.

Current conventional wisdom suggests the more FaceBook fans you have, the more people you have available to help spread your company's message - and the faster you will grow. This is the key belief in social media marketing circles... but as Voltaire said "Conventional wisdom is unwise" There's hope in the potential ability to market to people who are already captivated by your brand that want your products.

All About Relationship Building

By building relationships are you trying to be all things to all people? A lot of the social media elite assumes all B2B'ers are marketing pioneers - have a history of telling business focused stories or as Dan Kennedy asserts "Use proven systems that work because pioneers end up with arrows in their back"

But the reality is social media marketing takes a lot of time, support staff who understand the business of their customers. You'll need a lot more time to and money to execute your social media "The theory is that social media supposedly injects customers directly into the marketing process where they can accelerate or extinguish the marketing process" - what a load of BS. "Customers have moved front and center because the social web has democratized publishing." Refer to Branson's preceding observation. More chattering voices online doesn't necessarily equal democratization - it means more chattering voices online that are well, chattering. Better to think of social media as an annuity that pays off continually over time... if that's true, given the current state of the economy, annuities are invested in public debt, bonds, and stocks, so they are just as risky... especially since we're heading towards financial armageddon.

Social media can be integrated into an overall marketing scheme. You have to decide if the return is great enough to warrant your time and attention.

But is all of this for naught??

There are over 900 million objects that people interact with on social media sites, pages, graphs, events, and community pages... which is why "awareness" and engagement aren't accurate metrics. Besides being vague, there's no way of really knowing if anybody is seeing what you do or reading all of your valuable content on Facebook, your corporate blog, or any other platform. Google chairman Eric Schmidt reports that more information is created on the internet in 48 hours today than all mankind from the beginning of time of until 2003.

"Awareness" and "Engagement" don't mean anything to anyone except the champions or "gurus" of social media marketing who promote them. Has anyone ever thought "who has the time to read all of my valuable content?" Businesses have become so obsessed with creating valuable and useful "free"content, they've lost sight of your purpose for being in business in the first place.

Social media is not much different than traditional advertising; nobody really knows for sure if they're ads are working or not, its just that's what your "supposed" to do. So if business is good after an advertising campaign, then wonderful, the ads worked. If business is bad after an advertising campaign, of course the ads take the blame.

Remember, offline matters more than online... I don't know if that will ever change. Your message, your market, your media (I'll explain more on these later) determine your business's success. This whole notion if you put something online people will somehow magically "see it" is about as reliable as having a full-page ad on the inside cover of Glamour. People may "see" it but will it resonate with them? It's no different than the difference between hearing and listening.

Did you know most YouTube videos go unwatched and most websites receive no visits.

Is social media for you and your business?

You previously read how to find out if FaceBook is worth your while as a business (and personally for that matter). But what about other social media outlets are they worth the time, effort, money, and extra resources to commit to? Let's find out.

Don't obsess over where your website ranks. Ranking search results are now based on your previous personal links. Google provides search results based on what you clicked whether you are logged in or not. The location you're searching from, ip address provides location focused results even without the location in the search phase. Considering other factors like friends and recommendations from social media and your Google search ends up resembling shopping on Amazon. This kind level of customization makes key word irrelevant.

Unfortunately, most social media gurus recommend building a community of active sharers or your company's content on social media instead of focusing on search engine rank. In either case, you'd be better off offering an e-zine, newsletter, PDF special report, something they have to opt into so you can get their contact information and continue marketing to them.

6 "BUT THAT'S HOW EVERYBODY DOES IT"

"The minority is sometimes right; the majority is always wrong."

George Bernard Shaw

When Was the Last Time You Received a Hand Addressed Envelope in the Mail?

Traditional media's results are just as unreliable as digital media's

Social media, the internet, web marketing and even traditional marketing painfully illustrate how woefully ineffective 98% of all types of marketing really are... poorly written "creative" ad copy that doesn't connect how your product or service will solve a problem for your prospect, and little if any attempt to get contact info, leaving **you**, the business owner, VP of Marketing or the CEO holding the bag and wondering if what you're paying for will finally bring the results you've been waiting for as long as you've been in business.

The Power of Direct Response Marketing

Direct response marketing is so powerful because you market to a specific audience, appeal to them emotionally how they'll benefit using your product or service and ask them to take some form of action either to buy or send or download a free report. Either way, your persuading your prospect to commit to the idea of what you're selling. But the real power is your ability as the marketer, to test to see which of your marketing messages are effective and which ones you can toss. No more spending a Kings Ransom on a marketing campaign without knowing before hand is it even has a chance of working.

Another beauty of direct response is once a campaign is proven effective, you can pretty much keep running it until it stops generating revenue for you. I know of one campaign that ran in a popular golf magazine for eight years, making the company millions. It finally stopped pulling and was eventually replaced. You can create similar materials for your online marketing as well that generate new clients and new revenue over and over and over again. For those who are reading about these strategies for the first time, these marketing pieces are called "evergreen" because you don't have to change them. So you use the same marketing message, continually attracting new prospects and move them along you sales process.

Here's a question for you: Why does Google mail promotional postcards to entice small business owners to open an AdWords account? If you guessed "it's because direct mail is more effective", then you're right. Google in its early years bragged about being the new paradigm of marketing and direct mail was dead... everything will be going online, the future is here today. Well, things haven't worked out as planned and people still overwhelmingly respond to direct mail.

Get Your Prospects Individual Attention

I asked you earlier if you know who your best clients are and if you marketed to prospects who fit the same demographic as your ideal clients; remember 20% of your clients generate 80% of your revenue? Just making sure you were paying attention. There's a formula used by marketers and ad copywriters, perhaps you've heard of it, AIDA. It stands for Attention, Interest, Desire, and Action. Interrupting and stopping your prospects cold in their tracks, and enter the conversation that is already occurring in her mind - that's the impact you are striving to make. Usually, it will come in the form of a headline that promises a benefit your prospect craves, yet almost seems to good to be true that's finally revealed to them if they keep reading.

One of my favorite examples is legendary copywriter John Carlton's infamous "One Legged Golfer" headline. If you're a golfer, this ad would have sliced through all the clutter in your mind, ignite your curiosity and ultimately make you crave the product as if you were powerless to prevent yourself from opening your check book and writing a check payable to OHP Golf, LLC. Here it is... tell me how it makes you feel, especially if you're a golfer.

Amazing Secret Discovered By One-Legged Golfer Adds 50 Yards To Your Drives, Eliminates Hooks and Slices... And Can Slash Up To 10 Strokes From Your Game Almost Overnight!

Wow!!! This is perhaps one of the most ripped off headlines ever. I know what you're probably thinking "Yes, but that guys a copywriting legend, I could never write like that and I'm not sure I want to." You're right.... you probably could never master sales writing like John Carlton. But the good news is you *don't* have to. You can quickly develop enough skill to implement or have a member of your staff implement to see a dramatic boost in response to your marketing efforts.

Even if you practice writing headlines for a month, then you will begin to develop your mindset to see the benefits of doing business with your company from your clients point of view.When you learn to tap into how your product or service can solve the problems that keep your client lying in bed at night, unable to sleep because of anxiety, then now you're getting somewhere.

Several years ago I owned a real estate investment company. It was right about the time people's property values were plummeting like a thermometer on a cold day. I had 10,00 flyers distributed to my identified neighborhoods throughout the county that fit my criteria for buying houses. The AIDA formula fit brilliantly here. The first step, attention, was achieved by the design of the flyer itself. Resembling a UPS notice stuck on the front door of the house, it immediately got attention because everybody wants to see who sent them a package from UPS. Now the prospects interest was stoked when they pulled the Sticky-Note off their door and read *"Sell your house, As-Is, for a fair price, on the date of your choice"* At that point, the homeowner is either in or out. They were either in a position where they needed to sell or they were content and they had no interest in selling there home. Desire was stimulated when they further read my encouraging and hopeful message of a possible way out of their financial mess by providing a solution that know one else could provide for them - if they qualified.

And action was encouraged by asking them to call a 24-hour toll free number with a recorded message explaining exactly the program I had and how it could potentially benefit them. At the end of the recorded message, I instructed prospects to go to my website, fill out a diagnostic survey so I can assess their needs and see if they qualify. Notice the one thing I'm <u>not</u> doing here, communicating with prospects. No phone calls, no emails, no running around town for appointments UNTIL they are qualified.

I implemented systems to prevent the gigantic time suck of answering ordinary questions and talking to people who aren't qualified.... if you don't have systems in place to deal with this, all of the unimportant minutia will swallow up your time so fast, Friday will have arrived before you figure out you didn't accomplish one thing all week. Avoid it like the plague.... not only will you suffer, but it be catastrophic for your business.

StayingPower - Simple Ways to Stay in Your Prospects Mind

So then how do you keep in contact with your clients if you have a system to screen them, educate them on your products and services and they qualify but for some reason aren't 100% sold? Newsletters are an excellent way for clients to get to know you as well as an opportunity to let your personality show through. It's not just for the personal practice like a dental or medical office. Different staff members can contribute their weekly or monthly observations on their specialties that would both benefit and entertain clients. Send an enewsletter every week or two and paper/hardcopy letter monthly. The reason for the hardcopy is that its physical, they have to put it somewhere so your name is in front of them longer, reminding them of your existence. Remember out of sight, out of mind? Well a physical newsletter in their hands every month reminds them you're still kickin' and still have plenty of value to provide.

Holiday promotions are a great overlooked opportunity to connect with your clients. There's always some holiday being celebrated or observed every month. Who cares if its something like Arbor Day. You have an excuse to contact and connect with your client and to do so in such a way monthly that makes you not only stand out, but shows your human side to your clients. People buy from other people... not stodgy, cold, impersonal corporate images.

Corporate marketing doesn't sell. It only pacifies timid board members and inflates egos of the CEO and upper management involved in the decision. For example, during my stint as a financial advisor, the firm I represented, (as well as all firms in the securities industry) were overly cautious about what we could say in letters, brochures, pamphlets, investment advice... etc. Naturally, they had to follow the law and certainly I understand that. So they had pre-approved marketing online and all I had to do was insert my name and voila... a semi-custom marketing piece was ready for my disposal. But like most corporate advertising - boring. The compliance department wasn't interested in helping with my plight either. So I could use their pre-approved templates or nada. The corporate big wigs, on the other hand, had no problem spending Tens of Thousands of dollars to splatter the company name on the stadium of the local NFL franchise. As I recall, the name was prominently displayed on the roof of the stadium so the blimp camera shot wouldn't miss it. Which makes about as much sense as Goodyear having a blimp.

I think that's reminiscent advertising. You go to the big game with your family, everyone's having a great time, and there, up in the sky is the Goodyear Blimp.... I'm starting to tear up. So the reasoning goes, the next time you're in the market for tires, Goodyear is hoping you'll recall those fond memories you had at the game with your family, and choose to purchase their tires for your car. Hope is not a strategy.

Strategic Targeting - One Size Doesn't Fit All

So once you have identified your 20% of clients that generate 80% revenue how do you get more of them? You find out everything you can about them. Where they shop, what they eat, where they live, the price of the home they live in, the kind of car they drive, what magazines do they subscribe to, club memberships etc. Then you can create a specific message to one segment of your list. For example, say 27% of your prospects subscribe to Food and Wine Magazine. You can then create an ad campaign to all of those people by relating your product and service to Food & Wine Magazine. Say you offer a premium to the first 25 respondents that make an appointment to meet with you. The premium could be anything to tie the prospect to you and something they enjoy - a set of crystal red wine glasses, a serving tray set, a mixer, something like that. Finding high quality premiums that add value to your clients is not as expensive as you might think. And one thing's for sure; your competition isn't doing.

The danger with a "one size fits all" marketing message is that it will appeal to nobody. That's what corporate America does. Your job is to find who your best clients are, what keeps them awake at night and how you can fit your service to be their solution to what keeps them awake at night.

7 YOUR PROFIT REVOLUTION

"If you don't know where you are going, you might wind up someplace else."

Yogi Berra

Remember... Everyone Else Hasn't Got a Clue Either

The one secret, when revealed, accepted, learned and implemented, that guarantees your amazing success beyond your wildest dreams. In fact, failure to master this one secret, means your business, no matter what business your in be it manufacturing, software, doctor, lawyer, Fortune 500, butcher, baker, and candlestick maker ALL.... I repeat ALL businesses have to master this in order to survive. So what is it this ability???? The Ability to *Sell*. And not just sell, but sell with unabashed pride and honor, not with meek embarrassment. Nothing happens until somebody sells something. I'll even go out on a limb and say if you have a product or service that can help someone benefit in some way in their life and you can provide them with that benefit then it is your moral obligation, your duty to see to it that prospect willingly and cheerfully buys what you have. Your business, no, all businesses need to excel at selling. Selling and marketing are the masters, all others are the servants.

A case in point, Dan Kennedy, recalls a story where he was consulting for a Fortune 500 company. One day while working on site, the CEO called him into his office and said he revealed something startling to Dan. "I was going over how much we pay you, and I found you're getting paid more than I am and I'm the CEO." "Yes" Dan replied, "you're right... I am getting paid more than you are and there is a very important reason why I get paid more than you. You are the best person at managing, short-term goals, long-term goals, implemented and launching plans, and making sure the company runs well. No doubt about it you are better than anybody else doing that around here. But I know how to get clients, which you don't know how to do. Without clients, all those other functions you're the best at, couldn't exist. We'll just keep this as our little secret." And with that he got up from his seat and left the CEO's office. The CEO, by the way, never questioned him about his fees again during the entire time of the project.

Focus - Becoming Objective and Outcome Oriented
Over fifteen years ago, I had the unique experience of teaching GED courses to detainees in the Broward

County Main Jail in Fort Lauderdale, Florida. My students were not just any students... they were sexual offenders. That reason alone meant they were separated from other prisoners. They had their own floor or group of pods; they could not mix with general population detainees.

I learned in the jail, and in prison, there's an unwritten code of "honor" amongst criminals. No crimes against women or children. If you're in the slammer for a sexual offense, you'd better watch your back. The most frightening thing about this population was that these guys were intelligent, easy to talk to, and smooth... very smooth.

Except for one....

Emilio. He was a "Marielito", meaning he came to the US when Castro opened his jails in 1980 and a large chunk of Cuba's convicted felons, made their way to our shores, leaving from the port city Mariel. I had my own nickname for Emilio too; *Nitro-Glycerin Man*. I never called him that to his face, he was just that unstable. Incidentally, Emilio was in jail for murdering his estranged wife on live TV with his .357 magnum. And, according to Emilio, it was her fault.

Of course it was.

You might be wondering what a story about a sexual offender with some notoriety in South Florida has to do with your business.... let me explain.

You see, Emilio was in prison in Cuba for attempting to assassinate Fidel Castro, by his account anyway. I had to bite my lower lip to keep from laughing out loud when he told me this. In a thick accent he described "A lonnnng line of cars come down road. I

take bomb, throw under car and BOOOOOOOOM........
So what happened ? I asked. He shrugged his shoulders and simply said "wrong car." Whether the story is true or not, I'll never know and I'm sure the Cuban government won't verify it. Oh, and he said the reason he was spared the death penalty is Cuba's capital punishment laws effect people 19 years and older... he was 18. Not that believable, I know, but here's the main point:

If Emilio's story is indeed true, what one thing would have prevented him from selecting the wrong car that could also be impacting your business? Now I wasn't there but if you're trying to assassinate your nation's leader, I'd be willing to bet the reason he failed just might have been a lack of focus.

Do you have focus in your business? Are you focused on monthly production goals? Are you focused on your marketing with different messages to each of your most profitable niches? Are you focused in providing a positive and rewarding client experience consistently every time?

Most business just get by, by trying to be all things to all people. There's no consistency between marketing message, how clients are treated, to how calls are handled.

My favorite instance of this is when you buy or lease a new car. Within the first 3 weeks, somebody calls me to see how I liked the service at the dealer and what my overall satisfaction level was. You ever get one of these calls? So the one time they called and I had a complaint about the service you what the caller on the other end of the line said? "Well we're not the dealer, we just make the calls and record the responses" So here after several leases and purchases I thought I was getting a nice "thank you for your business is everything o.k. call" but in reality the dealer, I'm not sure what the dealer was getting from it because nobody ever called me back. HUGE credibility killer. Its one of the reasons why people don't trust what they here or see in marketing. They've heard it all, seen it all, and they've come to expect a business or person won't do what they say they're going to do. Too bad, really. But an excellent opportunity for you to out serve your competitors.

The One Question Ad Agencies and Social Media Gurus Hate to Answer...

Because They Can't

One way you can tell if an ad agency, web or SEO consultant is effective in bringing in clients is to ask them the same question you would ask an investment advisor. I got this idea from multi-millionaire and financial publisher, Mark Ford, of the Palm Beach Letter. It bears repeating here. He said there's only two questions you need to ask and have answers to when making an investment: How much will I earn? and when will I get paid? That's it. Now you might be thinking, "Hey Randy that's great investment advice, I'll try to remember that the next time I get a call from my broker." Here me out.

An effective, targeted and well crafted sales letter that evokes strong emotions is worth it's weight in gold. I know I mentioned this earlier but what you're actually doing is creating an asset you can use over and over and over again. So many businesses cut corners and try to take the cheapest way out - That's nuts. Do you cut the same corners on your personal investments, retirement, college savings for your children or grandchildren? And.... its completely ignorant to what really makes business run. Nothing happens until a sale is made.

So the next time an ad rep or social media guru or some whiz bang web designer tries to tell you that you need the latest marketing gadget or trend because everyone "else is doing it" or "you don't want to be left behind" say to them, "so if we go ahead with your service today, what kind of return will I get, and how quickly will I see results" If they come up with any answer that says that ROI is not important, or every time ROI is mentioned, "a unicorn dies", it takes time to build your brand .... yadda, yadda, yadda, run and run quickly.

How to Lemming Proof Your Business and Marketing

So what can you do to keep your business from looking, sounding, and marketing like all the chattering noise that's already out there? How do you insure that you don't become caught up in the masses of online marketing lemmings heading over the cliff? I'll keep it basic repeating some of things we spoke about earlier and build upon from there.

1. What business are you really in? You're not in our's is the biggest, best, oldest, whatever business. (Hint: You're in the marketing business)

2. What emotional problem does your product or service solve?

   a. A dentist doesn't just fix broken teeth, she can give you more self confidence with a new, sexy smile.

b.   An accountant doesn't just keep books and file tax reports, she can eliminate the headaches and cold sweats by keeping your business IRS audit free.

c.   A landscape architect and contractor doesn't just put new plants in your yard, he creates a relaxing, peaceful, and beautiful new space that you enjoy coming home to and are proud to have your friends over. Do you see where I'm going with this? It doesn't matter what business you're in, you will be safer

3. Why your client need to buy your service right now, if you need to be compelling and urgent... and if they're not ready, "touch" them with weekly emails or direct mail so they don't forget you are the person that can help them.

Just acknowledging and thinking about the above three questions will begin to make you more aware about your business than all of your competition and 90% of all businesses out there, period. But you have to implement and act. The next section will give you a primer as to what you can do to begin to take your business to the next level.

You Already Have the Tools, Because You Know Your Business Better than Anybody.

Once you have the questions to last section section answered you can apply the basic building blocks of marketing. They're the same no matter what business your in. In fact, you may have seen what I am about to show you before. If you have seen this before and blew it off because it seemed like a lot of work, or that's not what the local ad reps do or I didn't learn this in business school, then listen up bucko, because its not too late to jump into the game.

There are three key parts to your marketing that every business owner has to have in their marketing or their marketing campaigns will fail miserably. They are your message, your market, and your media.

Your Message - As we spoke about earlier, what's your Unique Selling Proposition or your elevator speech that gets right to point of how what you do, immediately benefits your prospect. For instance, FedEx's is "When It Has to Absolutely, Positively be There Overnight"

There's not much wiggle room in that message is there? We already mentioned Domino's Pizza but how about there competitor Papa Johns? "Better Ingredients, Better Pizza, Papa Johns" Naaa, it sounds too much like "me too." People don't care about fresh ingredients as much as they care about getting their food fast. Look at Burger King.... everybody knows they have better food than McDonald's but McDonalds dominates them because they're fast. If you want good you go to someplace nicer, sit down service, where a server takes your order and brings you your food. You pay more, but hey, that's what YOU wanted.

There's a Dunkin' Donuts near my house that always blocked south bound traffic on U.S. 1 because cars waited to make u-turns to go back north to the Dunkin' Donuts drive through. Well wouldn't you know Starbucks, spotting an opportunity greater than alleviating traffic congestion for the City of Ft.

Lauderdale, moved the vacant building next door. What do you think happened to the Dunkn' Donuts? The simply switched from there to Starbucks. Now I don't mean that Starbucks captured all of DD's business but they made a sizable dent just by observing when I drive by in the morning.

Similar but opposite to the Burger King vs. McDonalds. McDonalds focuses on FAST and their prices are similar, maybe cheaper than BK's. Starbucks though, offers a whole "experience" that people are eagerly and patiently (even while caffeine deprived until their first cup) waiting in oftentimes long lines. Their employees are "Baristas", they have their own unique language for their beverages. There's a sense of smooth calm amongst the busy chaos in the shop. Dunkin' Donuts is more product oriented, tell us what you want and we'll give it to you... and they're definitely cheaper than Starbucks, but it ain't about the price.

If you haven't seen or heard comedian John Pinette's routine about long lines, I suggest you log on to YouTube and check it out. It's funny but really highlights the differences between Starbucks and Dunkin' Donuts and what people are willing to wait longer for, while paying higher prices.

Your Market - This bears repeating, who are your ideal clients? Not one's with just a pulse, your ideal clients? Are they short or tall? Wide or narrow? Wealthy or middle income? (I've only heard of one company, by the way, that intentionally targets low income consumers. FingerHut, a mail order firm that sells the basic sundries people use for everyday life. Like a mail order version of a Wal-Mart or Beall's. I worked with their former VP of Marketing and she shared with me the way they were able to be profitable catering to low income consumers was to extend credit on basic sundries, knowing they'd make their profit on the interest as it accrued... because their ideal client seldom had enough cash in a checking account to buy their products).

Where do they live, what do they drive, where do the dine out, what clubs do they belong to, are they young or old? Regardless, you want to make sure they can afford what your offering and your price point will allow you to make a profit to keep the doors open for your business.

Your Media - How you present your message to your market digital, print, video, direct mail....the vehicle you choose to deliver your message to your market is your media. As we've previously discussed, social media is just another type of media to deliver your message. It is not *the best or the only* way to deliver your message. People always want to know "what's the one thing I can do to increase my sales through my marketing?" There isn't one thing... no magic bullet to make it easier to eliminate all of your marketing challenges. Sorry. There are many types of media you can use effectively to consistently deliver your message all contributing to your revenue if you've properly identified your market and written a compelling message they can benefit from.

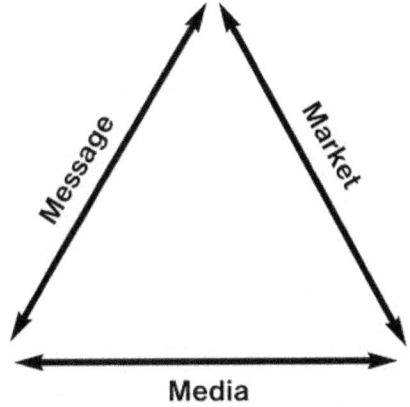

The 3 Sides of the Marketing Triangle

In the marketing triangle above, the message side is the "what" of your product or service. What is it you want me to see? What about your product or service is unique that will grab my attention and cause me to stop what I'm doing to see what you have to offer? What does your product or service do for me?

The market side of the triangle is the "who" of your marketing. Who is your ideal client? The more specific the better. If your product is competitive dogsleds, make sure you aren't targeting your message to RV owners over the age of 65.

The bottom portion or the media portion of the triangle is the "how." How are you going to deliver your message to your market? What vehicle are you going to use? Print, digital, direct mail, email. Which media will get the most exposure for you in front of your target audience?

8 STEP BACK, TAKE A DEEP BREATH.... NOW DIVE IN HEAD FIRST

"Everywhere is within walking distance, if you have the time."

Steven Wright

You've just read and absorbed a lot of information. Some of it you're familiar with but most of it is probably new to you. It sounds good, like its worth trying to see how it compares to the way your currently attract clients. But where should you start.

First and foremost you need to identify what business you're really in. This is the most difficult step because most of us get our sense of identity through what we do for a living. I'm a doctor, lawyer, teacher, paramedic, CEO, human resources director etc. We pride ourselves on what we do and identify with it as who we our. I used to do it to.... in fact, after tell someone my

USP, I'll often follow up with "I'm a strategic marketing consultant and sales copywriter." It's a dramatic shift in thinking of yourself differently than the way everyone views what they really do. Transitioning from the "doer" of the thing to the "marketer" of the thing is an adjustment. Ultimately, your goal is to reach somewhere in the neighborhood of 60% strategic planning and marketing to 40% of actual "hands-on" involvement.

Coincidentally, or not so coincidentally, great business leaders and coaches like Napoleon Hill, Earl Nightingale, Jim Rohn, and Dan Kennedy all reveal that spending more time "on" your business than "in" your business is a key foundation to phenomenal success no matter what your vocation. I stumbled and struggled with this until my first successful marketing launch for real estate clients in 2005. Prior to that I was feeling probably similar to some of you, wondering if this marketing "stuff" really works. As soon as I my marketing "hit" my prospects, my automated recording and electronic application systems were overwhelmed... I couldn't handle the surge in volume. I was pleasantly dumbfounded. Hmm, "this 'stuff' not only works, but works beyond anything I imagined!" I thought.

Once you accept what business you're really in, you need to do some business intelligence work and figure out who are the 20% of your clients that generate 80% of your revenue. What keeps them awake at night? What problem of theirs do you or your product solve for them on an *emotional* level? Find out what makes them tick. Learn everything you can about them.

Why? Because your identifying the key factors and character traits of your best clients, so you can effectively find and market to prospects who have the same profile, or psychographic, that your best clients have. Once you have that information, you can obtain a list matching the psychographics of your target market and market to them.

Next, once you know who your ideal client is and what keeps them awake at night in nervous, anxious sweats, then you create your USP specifically to identify their problem and how you'll be able to solve that problem for them. There are several ways people use to create a USP and/or your Elevator Speech. I prefer the one from copywriting legend John Carlton. It's simplest and most direct. It goes something along these lines -

1. Who - Who or what group of people you help

2. What - what benefit do they get by using you.

3. How- faster, cheaper, easier, less stress, etc.

4. Whatever - your situation, income, revenue, etc.

In a paragraph, it would look something like this:

> We help (this group of people) ... with, do, get (this benefit) ... (better, faster, easier, cheaper, stress reducing) ... whatever, even if (worst case believable scenario).

That's it, in a nutshell. A little practice and elbow grease and you'll be crafting some powerful USP's in no time. Again, I didn't create this formula for writing your USP. John Carlton did.

You're halfway home to creating great, compelling sales messages.... messages that are effective both online and offline that are "evergreen." They can be used over and over and over again. Writing your sales and marketing messages can be done by you or you can hire a strategic marketing consultant or copywriter to help you if its something you don't want to tackle.

Good sales copy follows a formula that can be replicated once learned. It won't happen overnight though; it will require practice. All good sales messages contain a:

> a.) Headline that stops your prospect dead in their tracks
>
> b.) Subhead that reinforces the headline stimulating curiosity to continue reading.
>
> c.) Body that tells your story of who you are, what it's in it for them, and why your prospect needs to act quickly!
>
> d.) Proof, proof, and more proof, will be used in the body to build your case why the prospect needs your product or service.
>
> e.) p.s. and a p.s.s. are your last two chances to sell your client. After the headline, your prospect will jump down to the end of your message to see who sent it. The p.s. and p.s.s. magnetically draw their eyes to the copy.
>
> f.) a compelling offer that is believable and beneficial to your prospect and completely risk-free for your prospect.

After your message is crafted, you need to choose which media or what combination of media that will generate the best results. Remember the most dangerous number in business is one. You owe it to the survival of your business to have more than one way or type of media for your prospects and clients to receive your message. Offline would include:

> 3-page sales letters to targeted lists
>
> advertorials - sales letters that look like news articles
>
> post cards
>
> flyers
>
> monthly specials tied into a holiday that month (the more obscure the holiday, the better)
>
> TV Infomericals
>
> Radio
>
> seminars
>
> public speaking

Online would include:

> Email - sideways sales letters
>
> webinars
>
> teleseminars
>
> landing pages
>
> sales pages

Avoid at all costs the mindset of getting the "cheapest marketing" and learn to embrace the idea of testing marketing that is effective and generates you revenue, even if it is expensive while earning you a profit.

Beware of the temptation to "build your brand" if you are just starting out or as previously mentioned, you have internal issues that need addressing first. The problem I see with brand awareness is too many businesses focus on making people aware of their brand rather than getting clients and have their brand evolve naturally as a result of great marketing and exceptionally unexpected client service not only when the sale is made, but long after, prompting your new clients to remark how amazingly different you are and how much fun it was to do business you.

When Donald Trump was breaking into the Manhattan real estate development market, he took on a project that helped him build his brand, as a result of what he did, not before he did it.

"In the 1980's I watched the Wollman Rink in Central Park getting renovated for six years with nothing getting done. I finally offered to help and had it done in a few months. I suddenly had a big reputation as a guy who gets things done - on time and under budget. People couldn't believe it could be done but I know better. Build your reputation around getting things done."

Studying Trump is an excellent way to learn how he's evolved his brand by offering unmatched service and quality and intuitively realizing consistency in providing the best for his clients. He hasn't really put himself "on the hook" because he committed and truly believes in only offering the best. After several decades, he has earned such a high degree of trust no marketing campaign could ever create, manufacture, and promote effectively.

You'll also have to learn (if you haven't already done so by now) to develop an immunity to criticism...

because its coming whether you realize it or not. I've learned when I set out to do something that most people wouldn't dream of doing or set goals that are higher than most people, you will most certainly face ridicule and doubt from "well-meaning" family and friends. Some people, like family members, may think their intentions are good but usually they're not. In fact, they can be crippling if not demoralizing. Discount anyone else's criticism as their insecurity and fear of stepping out of the "norm" and fear of being criticized by others.

Sadly, most people you associate with only want you to succeed as long as you don't accomplish or have greater success than they have - whatever that is. I became a billionaire at 23, the money just hasn't shown up yet. I related this to a woman I knew expressing my desire to be a billionaire and she just stared at me blankly, as if to say "why on earth... you couldn't do that."

Its harder to let go of critical people especially if they're family and really close friends. Case in point; when I was in middle school, I learned how to fly fish. Along with learning how to cast I learned how to tie my own flies as well. Once I had tied several patterns I excitedly proclaimed to my father, "Dad, I can go around to the bait & tackle shops on my bicycle and sell my flies." Thinking my dad would share in my excitement he replied, "yeah but Randy, you can't make any money doing that."

BOING!!!

I was only in 7th grade! Fortunately, I didn't listen to him and proceeded to pedal my way around to all the bait & tackle shops that were close to my house, which there were only 3, and only one of which bought my flies to sell for their customers.

More recently, I broke one of my cardinal rules of business: Never do business with family and friends and if you do, for God's sake don't offer your services to them for free. A couple of months ago, a friend of mine for over 20 years and the best man at my wedding, called and asked me for my professional opinion by looking over a proposal for him from a web design and seo consulting firm. Not a problem... and after reviewing the proposal I recommended he not go ahead with the consultants he was considering, saving him, by the way, $5000 big ones. He never called or emailed me to say thank you, by the way.

Several weeks later he anxiously called and asked if I could "spruce up" a reply page for his website because he was getting a lot of inquiries from a domain name he recently purchased for his wholesale food business and didn't feel confident with what his current marketing piece. So I did what any strategic marketing consultant would do, I looked it over, made great recommendations that were designed to boost response rates and sent it back with a quote. He emailed me back saying "thanks, but that's more than I want to pay." No big deal, right? Wrong!

Several days later I get a call from him saying he had a problem with my price (which I discounted for him because of our long friendship) and thought it was too high given the assignment he thought and the length of time my company had been established. According to him, I didn't have the "credentials" to justify such a high price. Never mind I've been doing this in such diverse fields as real estate, education, fund raising, finance, and publishing since 2004, he was peeved because the price was too high which was a discounted by two-thirds because he was a longtime "friend."

It suddenly dawned on me during our conversation that he didn't have a problem with my "credentials" when I saved him $5000 big ones a few weeks earlier. I let him have it. In his mind, the more the price dropped, the higher my credential climbed. Is that government thinking or what? But the important thing to get from this: some people will always have a problem paying for quality service and then wonder why things aren't going smoothly with their transactions and in their business. Avoid people who try to chisel you for every last dime or negotiate strictly by bottom line. Like Dr. David earlier in this book, they waste your time and have a negative effect on your psyche. You don't need unappreciative people in your life both in business and in your personal life as well.

Other peoples fears and lack of relevant experience keep them from seeing the big picture; its not the money, as they see it, but the experience in helping people solve their problems that leads to getting paid really well. More importantly, its the person you become. Everybody has their stuff they have to work out, but money is one issue that effects everyone, all the time. Most people don't have a clue how to make any, so they will be of little support or of little value to you when you embark on that journey yourself. Remember the ancient Japanese proverb: "a fool and his money, will soon part"

Immunity to criticism also applies when you begin to explore new ways of marketing, like direct response marketing. Ad reps, web and seo consultants won't "get" what you're trying to accomplish because they have not been taught direct response marketing and copywriting.

I hope this little book is catalyst to start you on your way to learning more about how to dramatically increase your profits, helping more people, turning a deaf ear to the nay-sayers you will surely encounter, and have more fun in your business when learn what really works in marketing and sales.

Besides yourself, you owe to your prospects and clients to fulfill your moral obligation to attract and sell them your product or service only if it will improve their health, wealth, life, and business. Good luck and remember... *Help more people, make more money, have more fun!*

THE MARKETING CONTRARIAN'S RESOURCE GUIDE

1. DIRECT RESPONSE MARKETING, SALES COPYWRITING, CONTRARIAN BUSINESS SAVVY

A.) DAN KENNEDY   WWW.DANKENNEDY.COM

B.) JOHN CARLTON   WWW.MARKETINGREBEL.COM

C.) DONALD TRUMP   WWW.DONALDTRUMP.COM

D.) RICHARD BRANSON WWW.VIRGIN.COM

E.) JIM ROHN   WWW.JIMROHN.COM

D.) MARK FORD   WWW.PALMBEACHLETTER.COM

2. ONLINE AND SOCIAL MEDIA MARKETING

A.) GOOGLE ADWORDS AND FACEBOOK MARKETING
PERRY MARSHALL   WWW.PERRYMARSHALL.COM

B.) SEO MARKETING   WWW.PLANETOCEAN.COM

C.) GENERAL SOCIAL MEDIA   WWW.LIKEABLE.COM

D.) DIRECT MARKETING STRATEGIES
ANDREW CASS   WWW.ANDREWJCASS.COM

E.) TWITTER, LINKEDIN, MANDE WHITE
WWW.MANDEWHITE.COM

ABOUT THE AUTHOR

Randy Gappen is a strategic marketing consultant and sales copywriter. Referred to as the man who creates "Marketing that Works," he's developed a 7-Step System helping frustrated businesses create easy-to-implement, hyper-effective solutions that not only "blow-the-doors-off" timid, traditional marketing, but are measurable, accountable, and almost instantly profitable.... guaranteed! He lives in Fort Lauderdale, Florida with his daughter and son.

www.RANDYGAPPEN.com